A Pod of
Whales

Heinemann Library
Chicago, Illinois

Richard and Louise Spilsbury

Customer Service 888-454-2279

Visit our website at www.heinemannlibrary.com

Designed by Ron Kamen and Celia Floyd
Originated by Dot Gradations Ltd
Printed in Hong Kong, China by Wing King Tong

07 06 05 04 03
10 9 8 7 6 5 4 3 2 1

Library of Congress Cataloging-in-Publication Data

Spilsbury, Louise.
  A pod of whales / Louise and Richard Spilsbury.
     p. cm. -- (Animal groups)
Summary: Describes the physical characteristics, behavior, habitat, and life cycle of whales.
  ISBN 1-4034-0743-6 (HC)   1-4034-3286-4 (PB)
  1. Whales--Juvenile literature. [1. Whales.] I. Spilsbury, Richard, 1963- II. Title.
  QL737.C4 S63 2003
  599.5--dc21
                          2002004035

Acknowledgments

The author and publishers are grateful to the following for permission to reproduce copyright material: p. 4 Oxford Scientific Films; p. 5 A.N.T./NHPA; p. 6 Kitchin and V. Hurst/NHPA; p. 7 Stephen Krasemann/NHPA; pp. 8, 16 Doc White/BBC Wild; p. 9 National Marine Mammal Laboratory; p. 10 Tui De Roy/Oxford Scientific Films; p. 11 Image Quest/NHPA; p. 12 Armin Maywald/BBC Wild; p. 13 Duncan Murrell/Oxford Scientific Films; p. 14 Howard Hall/Oxford Scientific Films; p. 15 Jeff Foott/OKAPI/Oxford Scientific Films; pp. 17, 23 Gerard Lacz/NHPA; p. 19 Pacific Stock/Bruce Coleman Collection; p. 20 Panda Photo/FLPA; p. 21 Brandon Cole/Nature Picture Library; p. 22 Jim Watt/Bruce Coleman Collection; p. 24 Minden Pictures/FLPA; p. 25 Gerard Soury/Oxford Scientific Films; p. 27 David Currey/NHPA; p. 28 Brandon D Cole/Corbis.

Cover photograph of humpback whales bubble-net feeding, reproduced with permission of BBC Wild/Brandon Cole.

The publishers would like to thank Claire Robinson for her assistance in the preparation of this book.

Every effort has been made to contact copyright holders of any material reproduced in this book. Any omissions will be rectified in subsequent printings if notice is given to the publisher.

Some words are shown in bold, **like this.** You can find out what they mean by looking in the glossary.

Contents

What Are Whales?

Whales are big **mammals** that spend their entire lives in the seas and rivers of the world. They have large mouths, small eyes, and nostrils called **blowholes** on top of their heads.

Whales are fantastic swimmers. Their arms, called **flippers**, are shaped like paddles. Whales have no legs, but at the end of their bodies they have wide, flat tail fins called **flukes**.

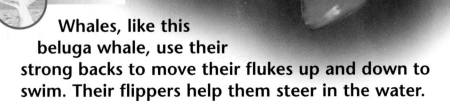

Whales, like this beluga whale, use their strong backs to move their flukes up and down to swim. Their flippers help them steer in the water.

Whales are not fish

Some people think that whales are big fish because they live in water, are fish shaped, and are good swimmers. But there are big differences. Whales, like other mammals, breathe air using lungs and give birth to young that they **suckle** and care for. Fish lay eggs and breathe using gills.

Are all whales the same?

There are 76 different **species** of whales. Scientists divide them into two groups. Toothed whales, such as orcas and sperm whales, have rows of teeth. **Baleen** whales, such as humpback whales, have tough fringes, called baleen, attached to their upper jaw instead of teeth.

Humpback whales have long, bumpy flippers.

Colors and patterns

Whales differ greatly in size and appearance. Many species are different shades of gray, but the blue whale is blue. Dolphins, which are also part of the whale family, vary from gray to pink. Others, such as orcas, have patterns of stripes, spots, or blotches of different colors.

Life in water

Whales have several **adaptations** to help them live in water. They have smooth, hairless skin, and a very **streamlined** shape that helps them move through the water. They have a thick layer of **blubber** under their skin that keeps them from getting cold in the water. Blubber also helps whales float in the water.

Heavy land animals, such as elephants, need strong bones to support their weight. Even though whales are heavy, their bones are light, and the water they live in helps support their giant bodies.

What is a whale pod?

Each whale is an individual that spends some or most of its time alone, feeding or traveling. However, it is also usually a member of a group of whales of the same **species.** This group is called a pod.

Whales hold their breath for a very long time so they can stay underwater longer. These orcas have come to the surface of the water to breathe through their **blowholes.**

What Is a Whale Pod Like?

Every pod has a slightly different number of whales in it. Sometimes a pod is made up of one adult male whale accompanied by an adult female. Many pods are made up of one or more female whales and their young. These are called **nursery pods** and can contain up to 30 whales of different ages. **Bachelor pods** are pods that contain several adult or younger male whales.

This is a pod of belugas, a type of white-skinned, toothed whales.

Herds and schools

The whales in a pod travel around together. Sometimes several pods and individuals join to make larger groups, especially in places where there is lots of food. Bigger groups of **baleen** whales are often called herds, and bigger groups of toothed whales are called schools. Some schools of dolphins, a type of small whale, can reach tens of thousands of individuals.

Who is who in a pod?

For most groups of animals, there are times when a leader can be useful. The leader is sometimes called the **dominant** animal.

In some **nursery pods** of whales, such as those of the sperm whale, the oldest female is often dominant. She leads the younger animals to where food is and also to where males will be when it is time to **mate.** In a **bachelor pod**, the oldest, fastest, or strongest male sometimes leads the hunt for food.

Swimming in formation

● ● ● ● ● ● ● ● ● ● ●

Whales in pods sometimes swim in certain patterns. Dominant whales may swim nearer to the surface of the water than others in their pod. They might also swim at the front of a triangle-shaped traveling group.

Where Do Whales Live?

Many whale **species** can be found throughout the world's oceans. But some live only in certain areas of the world's seas or even in particular rivers.

Water world

Although the world's oceans might look the same on a map, one area of the sea can be very different from another. Areas of water near the equator are always warm. Areas near the Arctic and Antarctic are always cold. Other areas of water become warmer or cooler as the seasons change or as **currents** change. The temperature of an area of water is one of the most important things affecting what lives there.

Some whales have **adaptations** that allow them to live in particular areas. For instance, the bowhead whale that lives in cold Arctic waters has extremely thick **blubber** to keep it warm.

Blubber makes up 40 percent of a bowhead whale's body weight.

9

Living soup

When **currents** of warm water mix with the cold waters of the Arctic and Antarctic, a rich "soup" of **nutrients** moves to the surface. **Plankton** feed on this soup. Larger animals, such as **krill**, feed on the plankton. Many **baleen** whales visit these cold waters to eat huge amounts of krill.

Moving to eat

All whales are **predators**. They hunt and eat other animals, such as fish or squid. Each **species** of whale eats particular types of **prey**, some of which only live in certain places or live there only during certain seasons. Many whales **migrate** to reach their food.

Gray whales spend the summer months feeding in the Arctic Ocean. They then migrate about 6,200 miles (10,000 kilometers) to warmer waters, near the equator, where they **mate**.

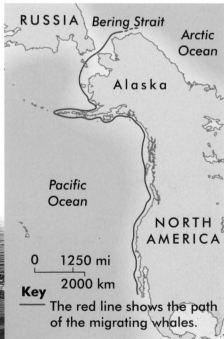

RUSSIA Bering Strait

Arctic Ocean

Alaska

Pacific Ocean

NORTH AMERICA

0   1250 mi

2000 km

Key

—— The red line shows the path of the migrating whales.

How Do Whale Pods Catch Their Food?

The two groups of whales—baleen and toothed—get their food in different ways. Baleen whales strain water through their baleen to catch the animals in it. Toothed whales use their sharp teeth to grab their prey.

Baleens eat a lot

Many of the largest whales are baleen whales. For most, the biggest prey they eat are less than four inches (ten centimeters) long, but they eat them in huge quantities. A group of krill can occupy an area the size of a football field and contain many tons of food.

On the fringe

Different baleen whale species have different kinds of baleen. A species called right whales have baleen made of fine bristles up to thirteen feet (four meters) long. These form a sort of mesh that can trap even tiny krill (shown magnified in the picture below). Minke whales have short, coarse baleen that trap only larger fish or squid.

Dinnertime

When they find an area of food, **baleen** whales use different methods to catch it. Some, such as blue and humpback whales, swim at **prey** and take a mouthful. Their grooved throats can stretch to hold enough water to fill hundreds of bathtubs. Closing their baleen, they push the water out of the sides of their mouths using their strong tongue and cheeks. Then they scrape off the food trapped on the baleen with their tongue and swallow it. A blue whale can swallow 4.4 tons (4 metric tons) of **krill** in one day.

Gray whales stir up mud on the seafloor using their jaws as plows. They then suck in the cloudy water, which contains shrimp, sea worms, and **mollusks.**

Southern right whales move along the surface with open mouths, sifting out their food as they swim along.

These humpback whales are **bubble-net** feeding. They work together underwater to blow rings of bubbles around schools of small fish. The fish, trapped in the bubble "net," swim to the surface. The whales follow, scooping up their prey as they go.

The sound of fast food

Toothed whales depend on their speed and teeth to catch fast **prey** such as fish and squid. They also use sound. They make special clicks and squeaks that send sound ripples through the water. When the ripples hit a school of fish, they bounce back as an echo and the whale hears how the sound has changed. The whale can then figure out where its prey is. This is called **echolocation**. Using this system, the whale can sense objects smaller than the head of a pin.

Deep sea diver

The sperm whale is the biggest toothed whale. It is 50 to 65 feet (15 to 20 meters) long. It hunts at depths of over one mile (about two kilometers). It can hold its breath for two hours, sometimes lying in the dark, waiting to surprise prey, such as giant squid and sharks.

Catching food together

Orcas usually hunt in pods of up to twenty whales. They surround prey and take turns attacking. Unlike other toothed whales, orcas eat seals, seabirds, and sea lions. They even attack great white sharks and large **baleen** whales. Some orcas work together to tip sleeping seals or penguins off floating pieces of ice so that other pod members can catch them.

Other toothed whales use special ways of hunting to get a good meal. Pods chase prey into water that is too shallow for swimming. The prey then head back to deeper water, straight into the waiting whales' mouths. One type of whale has even been known to steal tuna caught on fishing lines.

Some pods of orcas swim into the surf on beaches to catch sea lions. They have to time the waves right to avoid getting stuck on the sand.

Like other **mammals**, female whales spend a lot of energy having babies and caring for them. They tend to **mate** when there is a lot of food around. For many smaller whales, food is available year-round, so they can mate anytime. Large **baleen** whales can only use certain **feeding grounds** at particular times of the year.

Migrating and mating

Nursery pods of humpback whales fatten up in feeding grounds near the Arctic or Antarctic. Then they **migrate** to warmer waters to find males to mate with. After mating, they migrate back to the cold feeding grounds. They return to the warm **breeding grounds** a year later to give birth.

16

This humpback calf stays close to its mother.

Birth

Whale **calves** are often born tail first. Some calves are giants, weighing several tons. They are strong enough to swim right away. In the first minutes of life, a calf must take a breath of air. The mother, sometimes with help from other females in the **nursery pod**, nudges the calf up to the surface. This is called **supporting.** The calf's **blowhole** then opens for the first time in the air. Supporting continues until the calf can get the timing right, opening its blowhole only when it is above the water.

Feeding calves

A calf **suckles** from its mother soon after birth. Females produce hundreds of quarts of fatty milk a day. Suckling continues for six to eighteen months. After this time, calves will have learned how to catch their own food.

An orca calf can gain about two pounds (almost one kilogram) every hour and double its size in a week.

Growing up

In its first weeks, a young **calf** swims very near its mother. The mother protects her calf from **predators** by flapping her powerful **flukes** toward them.

Young whales in a pod learn a lot by watching their mothers and other adults. They learn how to swim faster and hold their breath long enough to dive deeper. They also learn special ways of catching food, such as **bubble-netting**.

Time to move on

Young whales are ready to **mate** when they are about five years old. Females often remain in the **nursery pods**, but males leave to join **bachelor pods**. In some **species**, such as sperm whales, males and females meet for only a few months each year to mate. They spend the rest of the year feeding in different parts of the oceans.

By swimming just behind its mother's **dorsal** fin, a humpback calf does not have as much **water resistance** to swim against. This means it does not get so tired.

How Do Whales Play and Rest?

As young whales grow up, they sometimes spend several hours each day playing. Some play is a gentle way of practicing skills they will use when they are adults. For example, by chasing one another, young toothed whales can practice their **echolocation** skills. By leaping out of the water, or **breaching**, a male whale can practice the skills that will be useful to show off to a future mate.

Whale play can also just be for fun, such as seeing how a feather or a stone sinks through the water. Both young and adult whales may play.

When humpback whales breach, they shoot out of the water and then slap back in with a loud crash.

Playful bachelors
● ● ● ● ● ● ● ● ● ● ● ● ●

One bachelor pod of sperm whales was seen body surfing in huge waves off South Africa. Another bachelor pod chased a male who was carrying a tree trunk in its mouth, like a dog with a stick!

Taking it easy

Swimming can be tiring, so many whales like to get help. Toothed whales sometimes do **bow riding** to save energy. While bow riding, they swim at a safe distance to the front and side of fast-moving boats. By tilting their **flukes** a certain way, they are carried along by the water pushed out of the way by the boat.

Whales may close their eyes and nap for up to two hours, sometimes while swimming slowly next to another whale. Whales may rest while floating horizontally or upright in the water. Whales prefer to rest near the surface so they can soak up the sun. They have to wake up regularly to go to the surface to breathe.

In some pods, one whale stays awake, on guard, while others sleep. Some dolphins can half-sleep. They shut down half their brain and close one eye. The side that is awake watches out for **predators.**

This sperm whale has closed its eyes to take a nap.

Do Whales Talk to Each Other?

Animals in groups **communicate**, or share information, about many different things. They may communicate information about food, how they feel, or what they want. They use hearing, sight, and touch to get information. Whales communicate mostly using sound.

Whales make low moaning sounds and short thumps or knocks, but also high-pitched chirps, whistles, and clicks. Some sounds are up to half a minute long, but others are much shorter. Fin whale moans can be heard from nearly 620 miles (1,000 kilometers) away.

Whales make some very loud noises. For example, blue whales can whistle louder than a jet engine.

Underwater talkers

Sound moves four times faster in water than in air and fastest in warm water. **Currents** of warm water carry some whale sounds for long distances. Because the whales cover large areas as they swim, they can communicate even when they are far apart.

Individual sounds

Each **species** of whale makes different kinds of sound. Whales listen for others of their own kind. They can also learn something about the individual who made the sound.

Whale sounds are made in tubes inside their heads. Larger whales have larger tubes that make different sounds than smaller ones. Many toothed whales **communicate** using whistles that are as individual as human voices. They whistle more often and faster when their pod is ready to hunt. Many **baleen** whales put together different sounds to produce long "songs."

Ocean musicals

When it is time to **mate**, a male humpback whale sings a song of grunts, groans, moos, and twitters that lasts up to 30 minutes. He then repeats his song exactly for hours on end, performing a kind of musical. Every male from one pod or **breeding ground** sings the same musical, but in an individual way.

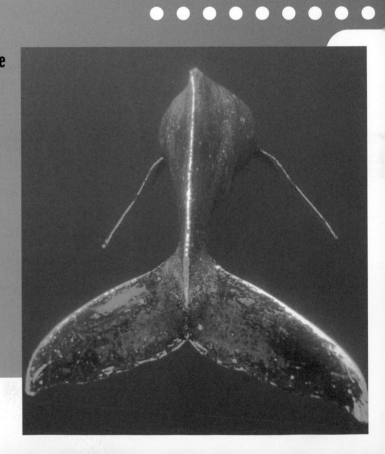

Amazing hearing

From underwater, captive dolphins can hear a teaspoonful of water being poured into a swimming pool and instantly locate where it is happening. Whales depend on sound not only for communication but also for **echolocation.** Hearing is their way of knowing the world around them. It helps them find out where **prey** and other whales are. It also helps them figure out the depth of water and the shape of the ocean floor.

Ears all over

The outer ears on the sides of the human head are only part of how a human hears. They collect the sounds, but it is the inner parts of the ear that help the brain understand what the sound is and where it came from. Whales feel sounds as tiny movements in the water around them with their sensitive skin. The sounds then move through their bones and fat to their ears, which are hidden inside, behind their jaws.

Whales have no need for outer ears, as they collect sounds all over their bodies. These sounds move to the hearing organs behind their jaws.

Do Whales Fight?

Whales in a pod get along with each other most of the time. However, when it is time to **mate**, tempers can flare, especially among whales in **bachelor pods.**

Each full-grown male sperm whale goes to its **breeding grounds** to try to become the **dominant** male. The dominant male gets the chance to mate with any female in the **nursery pod.** To become dominant, a male will have to prove to other males that he is stronger than they are. Males **display** by **breaching** and making loud noises by slapping their tails on the water or clapping their jaws shut.

Unicorn whales

● ● ● ● ● ● ● ● ● ●

Male narwhals have one long spiral tooth, called a tusk, which can be up to 8 feet (2.5 meters) long. Tusks are sometimes used to dig for food or to fight other males. But they are also a type of display. A long tusk shows others that its owner is strong and healthy.

Raking, butting, and biting

Displays are sometimes enough to frighten off other males, but often they turn into fights. Many male toothed whales use their teeth to scratch each other. The white lines on the backs of many beaked whales and gray dolphins are scars from being scratched.

Male sperm whales charge and butt each other with loud thuds. Sometimes they lock jaws and twist around in the water until one gives in and swims away, often with broken teeth and a bleeding mouth.

Battle for position

Male humpback whales fight to swim closest to a female they want to mate with. Each male tries to block the others by spreading its **flippers** wide, clashing **flukes**, or blowing trails of bubbles. Sometimes males lunge their knobby heads at each other.

Displays like breaching take a lot of energy. However, they are less harmful than getting in a fight would be.

25

One of the greatest dangers for a whale is drowning. Unless whales get to the surface of the water to breathe regularly, they will drown. If a pod member is hurt and cannot swim to the surface, others **support** it. Sometimes a sick whale will swim into shallow water so it can be sure of breathing. Often, the rest of its pod comes to join it, helping keep it upright until it either gets better or dies. However, sometimes the water is too shallow to get away, and whole pods can get stuck on beaches. This is called stranding.

Whale predators

The biggest whales are too huge for any sea animal **predator** to kill. Small, young, or hurt whales are most at risk from larger sharks or pods of orcas. Orcas, though not the biggest whales, have no natural enemies.

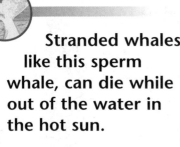

Stranded whales, like this sperm whale, can die while out of the water in the hot sun.

Whaling

In the past, people hunted whales for food. They also made things out of the whale bodies and sold these products to make money. At first, people hunted whales using hand-thrown harpoons or spears. Later, they used giant exploding harpoons. By the mid-1900s, there were very few whales of certain **species** left in the oceans.

This Norwegian whaling ship is shooting a harpoon at a minke whale.

In the 1980s, large-scale whaling was banned. But some countries still hunt whales. They say they do this to study whales, but often the meat is sold to restaurants.

Whale products of the past

In the past, margarine, shoe polish, makeup, soap, and lighting oil all contained whale oil made from whale **blubber**. Ribs for umbrellas and women's corsets that were fashionable 100 years ago were made from **baleen**. Whale meat used to be cheap and plentiful enough to feed to pets.

Other dangers

Thousands of whales die each year after being hit by ships or after being caught accidentally in fishing nets and then drowning. Whales, like all sea creatures, are also at risk from pollution. For example, chemicals dumped in the sea may poison them. Long-distance **communication** between whales is affected by noise pollution from ship engines. In some countries, orcas and dolphins are captured and kept in aquariums, where they are trained to do tricks.

Saving the whales

Conservation groups helped get large-scale whaling banned and have helped create protected areas for whales. Special airplanes that watch for whales can help ships to avoid hitting whales.

Whale-watching trips are a great way to get near whales in the wild. The more people know about whales, the more they will want to help protect them.

As long as boat owners don't get too close, whales are often very interested in people.

Whale Facts

Biggest and smallest

The blue whale is the largest living animal on Earth. When fully grown, it can be nearly 100 feet (30 meters) long—the same length as eight cars parked end-to-end. It can weigh 187 tons (170 metric tons), or about the same as 35 adult elephants. Its heart is the size of a small car and it pumps 11 tons (10 metric tons) of blood around its body. The smallest whale is the Chilean dolphin at just 3.9 feet (1.2 meters) long.

Slow going

Female whales usually give birth to one **calf**. Twins are rare. Females give birth at most every two or three years. This is one reason why whale populations increase very slowly.

Watching their backs

From a boat or from the shore, it is often tricky to identify a whale. After all, it only comes to the surface for a very short time to breathe. Here are some things to watch for:
- Blowing: Bowhead whales, for example, have double **blowholes** and blue whales create very tall spouts of water when they breathe out air.
- Fins, **flippers**, and **flukes:** Bowhead whales, for example, have no **dorsal** fin; orcas have a fin up to 6.5 feet (2 meters) tall.

Strange noises

In the 1950s, enemy sailors using special underwater microphones listened for the engine sounds of each other's submarines. They heard lots of strange noises. Scientists discovered these were the sounds of whales communicating through the water.

Glossary

adaptation   special feature that allows living things to survive in their particular surroundings

bachelor pod   group of male whales

baleen   hard, hair-like fringes attached to the upper jaw of baleen whales

blowhole   whale's nostril, located on top of its head. Some whales have two blowholes.

blubber   thick fat

bow riding   swimming helped by waves from a moving boat

breaching   leaping out of the water

breeding ground   special area where male and female whales meet to mate

bubble-netting   special way of hunting involving bubble-blowing that is used by humpback whales.

calf   (more than one are called **calves**) baby whale

communicate   pass on information to another

conservation   taking action to protect living things and the place in which they live

current   stream of water moving through surrounding still water

display   put on a show of actions that sends a message to another animal

dominant   refers to the leader or most important member of a group

dorsal   on the back of a whale

echolocation   the way in which toothed whales find objects using reflected sound

feeding ground   place with a good supply of food

flipper   front arm of a whale

fluke   whale's tail

krill   small shrimp-like animal

mammal   warm-blooded animal, such as a human or a whale. Mammal babies grow inside the mother. The mother cares for the babies after they are born and they drink her milk.

mate   joining of a male and female of the same species to create young

migrate   when animals move from one place to another far away

mollusk   type of animal that has a soft body, often protected by a hard shell, such as a clam

nursery pod   group of female whales and their young

nutrient   substance that animals eat to help them live and grow

plankton   tiny plants and animals that float or swim in water

predator   animal that hunts other animals for food

prey   animal that is hunted and eaten by another animal

species   group of living things that are alike in many ways and can mate to produce young

streamlined   describes something with a smooth shape

suckle   when a baby animal drinks its mother's milk

support   when one whale pushes another one to the surface of the water

water resistance   the force of water pushing against a swimming animal

More Books to Read

Carwardine, Mark. *Whales, Dolphins, and Porpoises*. New York: DK Publishing, 1998.

Facklam, Margery. *Bees Dance and Whales Sing: The Mysteries of Animal Communication*. San Francisco: Sierra Club Juveniles, 2001.

Greenaway, Theresa. *The Secret World of Whales*. Austin, Tex.: Raintree/Steck-Vaughn, 2001.

Holmes, Kevin J. *Whales*. Minnetonka, Minn.: Bridgestone Books, 1999.

Le Bloas, Renee and Jerome Julienne. *The Orca*. Watertown, Mass.: Charlesbridge Publishing, 2001.

Looking out for whales

If you see a stranded whale, do not touch it. Ask an adult to call the National Oceanic Atmospheric Administration's 24-hour hotline: 1-800-853-1964. They will help the whale if it is still alive. If it is dead, they will find out why it died. They study whale strandings to learn more about whales and how to best protect them.

Index